A Memoir of Faith, Family,
and Indigenous Identity

BEYOND BORDERS

Allison Kabildjanov MA TESOL

ISBN: 978-1-4866-2726-4
eBook: 978-1-4866-2727-1

Word Alive Press
119 De Baets Street Winnipeg, MB R2J 3R9
www.wordalivepress.ca

WORD ALIVE
—P R E S S—

Cataloguing in Publication information can be obtained from Library and Archives Canada.

LAND ACKNOWLEDGEMENT

I would like to take this opportunity to express my gratitude to the Treaty 1 territory and the traditional lands of the Anishinaabe (Ojibwe), Ininew (Cree), Oji-Cree, and Dakota, as well as the homeland of the Métis, where the Red River flows through—a place with a long history of trade between Indigenous Peoples and European settlers. This is where I reside with my family while writing this book.

CONTENTS

PREFACE   vii

Part 1: WINTER/PIPON
Chapter 1: EARLY YEARS   3
Chapter 2: TEEN YEARS   13
Chapter 3: COLLEGE YEARS   23
Chapter 4: LIFE IN CHINA   27

Part 2:SPRING/SĪKWAN
Chapter 5: RETURNING TO CANADA   43
Chapter 6: A GROWING FAMILY   47
Chapter 7: WORK AND LIFE   51

Part 3: SUMMER/NĪPIN
Chapter 8: TRIP TO THE STATES   61
Chapter 9: FINISHING STUDIES   65
Chapter 10: AFTER GRADUATION   67

Part 4: FALL/TAKWĀKIN
Chapter 11: DEALING WITH ANXIETY   75
Chapter 12: NEW CHALLENGES   79
Chapter 13: MOTHERHOOD   83
Chapter 14: FUTURE GOALS   87
EPILOGUE   89

PREFACE

I want to acknowledge my family and friends, as well as everyone I've crossed paths with, because without them, I wouldn't have the wealth of memories I'm able to share in this book. I am also forever grateful to and humbled before my Creator—God, or Kitchimanito in Oji-Cree, whom I found at a young age. Without my faith, I wouldn't have had the courage to serve Him.

The purpose of this book is to share a collection of stories depicting my journey as a young, energetic, and sometimes naive individual who fully trusted that God would care for me on my travels. I put my full trust in Him and was not afraid, for I saw my home as wherever my Creator God had placed me at that moment in time. This journey was not a decision I took lightly, and I did get lectured about my plans to "travel abroad" or "be a missionary." The risks of life overseas—getting sick or lost or having an accident—were real concerns, especially without the safety net of a hometown. My response was simple: I trusted in my Creator. And that was it—nothing could persuade me otherwise.

I also want to acknowledge some of the struggles I faced. Not all my choices were wise, and I made mistakes along the way. All of this has become part of my personal journey of self-discovery. It has also brought an awareness to the daily struggle with self-identity, which has been distorted by the historical impacts of colonialism on the minds of past and present Indigenous Peoples. I hope my story will bring healing, hope, and encouragement to the present generation of Indigenous Peoples.

— Miigwech / Thank you in Oji-Cree

Part 1
WINTER/PIPON

Chapter 1
EARLY YEARS

I was born in the small Canadian city of Thunder Bay on January 2, 1983. It was the coldest month of the year. Thunder Bay is located on the traditional lands of the Anishinaabeg, Ojibwe, Odawa, and Potawatomi Nations, where the traditional lands were surrendered under the Robinson-Superior Treaty, signed in 1850.

My parents are Virginia and Robert Kaminawatmin. Both of them are from northwestern Ontario, although not the exact same communities. Mom is Ojibwe and comes from a town called Red Rock, also located under the Robinson-Superior Treaty territories. Dad is Oji-Cree, from a town called Bearskin Lake First Nation, which is located in the Treaty 9 territories.

I was given the name Allison Katie.

Allison was the name of a nurse who cared for my mom throughout my birth. Mom didn't have visitors during her recovery at the hospital and felt really lonely. This nurse was exceptionally kind and caring and made an impression on her. Since Mom hadn't picked my name yet, she chose Allison in this nurse's honour. *Katie* was chosen after my father's late aunt who'd passed away early in life.

I was five pounds at birth and delivered via C-section. I was born with a dislocated hip, which my mom managed by adding extra diapers so my hip could correct itself. Thankfully the treatment worked and my hip eventually grew into its correct alignment. Otherwise I might have walked with a limp as an adult.

Our trip home from the hospital involved a long plane ride back to Mom's remote community. She later told me that she didn't have many baby blankets and that I was underdressed for the winter weather of the North. When my aunty first saw me, she said, "She must be cold!" I'm sure I looked like a half-frozen little bundle.

That weekend was busy with events surrounding the new year. The Canadian prime minister was on an eighteen-day trip to Asia to promote his country's exports. I've also learned that the movie *The Last Temptation* came out that weekend, and I now feel I'd like to watch it out of curiosity. Other than this, there wasn't much local news from Thunder Bay.

For the first two years of my life, I lived with both my parents and my elder brother in a small two-bedroom house in Bearskin Lake, Ontario. This is an Indigenous community located in the northwestern region of Ontario. The area mainly consists of forests, flatlands, and lots of swamps.

One of my earliest memories is of my first birthday. I remember sitting in a baby chair as many relatives came to visit. There are still photos of my aunts and older cousins as they sat around eating birthday cake. I even remember the Care Bears' birthday music playing in the background. I don't know where Mom found that music.

When I was a little older, my parents separated. I lived with Mom in Thunder Bay throughout my early school years.

One of my favourite toys was an Anne Shirley porcelain doll from my mom. When I was about eight or nine, I started reading the *Anne of Green Gables* book series, authored by Canadian writer L.M. Montgomery. I could also watch the *Anne* stories on TV back then. Around that time, a lady from the Big Sisters program gifted me a whole collection of *Anne* books because she knew I enjoyed reading. I'd been trying to impress her with my books, and it led to her buying me the whole *Anne* series.

The doll Mom bought was so pretty. She had braided red hair and a sun hat and wore a light-blue dress, just like the character in the movie series. I used to look up at that doll before bed and wish my life could be like Anne's—filled with adventures. Her bright-red hair, compared to my dark-brown, made me wish for something different than what I had. This doll represented everything I wanted to be—smart and dreamy, like Anne Shirley.

I eventually lost that Anne doll while moving around in my teen years, but I started collecting dolls again as an adult. This time, they were little Native American/Indigenous dolls, dolls that represented me with their dark-brown hair, dark eyes, and light-brown skin. Their facial features reminded me of the young girl I had always been.

In a way, the Anne doll had reminded me of what I wasn't. Growing up, I often felt uncomfortable with who I was and felt that others saw me differently, especially during my teen years.

Life with Mom left me feeling like an only child. I had an older brother but hardly saw him until I was in my late teens. By then, we were in completely different phases of our lives. Mom and I lived in a series of small apartments, and she didn't remarry. She was 5'1" with curly dark-brown hair and a medium build. Originally from the Nipigon/Red Rock area, Mom's childhood had been challenging as she'd grown up in foster care for most of her early life.

Mom came from a family of four siblings, two brothers and two sisters. She told stories about them when she was in the mood to talk, but beyond that, I didn't know her side of the family very well. One foster home in Thunder Bay stood out to her and left her with the most memories. She passed down her "white lady" voice and mannerisms to me, which I didn't even realize I'd picked up until my teenage years.

I took the school bus every day when I was young. I remember eating simple, healthy lunches like celery sticks and Cheez Whiz—nothing out of the ordinary. Some of Mom's favourite pastimes included baking, cooking homemade meals, visiting friends, and walking in the park.

I remember back in first or second grade, the teacher asked us to do daily journaling and draw a little picture to go with the story. Anyone could share their story with the class if it was interesting. One day, I wrote about Mom baking something and accidentally leaving a spatula in the oven. Instead of fresh baking, we ended up with a melted spatula. That was my story for the day, and my classmates all laughed because I drew a sad face next to the melted spatula.

Mom was a good cook though. At Thanksgiving, we always had turkey, potatoes, stuffing, and desserts. One dish I've never seen anywhere else was an orange Jello with shredded carrots— it's called orange gelatin salad. Apparently, it's an American dish from the Pennsylvania region. How it became part of our meals, I have no idea. For whatever reason, Mom made this dish with every turkey dinner and called it "salad." As an adult, I decided to carry on the tradition and make this Jello salad with my family's turkey meals.

Aside from that, Mom also made homemade pies entirely from scratch. I could never get the pie dough as crispy as hers. Eventually, I discovered you could buy ready-made pie dough and just roll it into the pie plate—that became my go-to method.

Growing up, Mom and I often took walks in the park with friends. Thunder Bay is a small city with a population of a little over 100,000 and is located on the western side of Lake Superior. As far back as I can remember, the parks were always beautiful, offering a view of Lake Superior and the Sleeping Giant. I still enjoy visiting the parks there, especially in the Port Arthur area, which is the north section of the city. On the north side is Marina Park, Boulevard Lake, and Centennial Park, boasting nearby rivers, beautiful scenery, and walking paths.

I remember once, in the middle of summer, we were walking in the International Friendship Garden, which contains monuments dedicated to a variety of countries—China, Portugal, Slovakia, and others. That evening, the sidewalk was covered in cankerworms (also known as army worms). There was a bad outbreak of them that year, and they had taken over the trees, spinning webs everywhere. The streets and sidewalks were piled with them, so our walk turned into a game of avoiding the worms, which was both challenging and gross. I did squish a few accidentally, but I hated the way it felt beneath my shoes. Later, I developed a fear of worms and began having nightmares about cankerworms.

Mom often performed random acts of kindness. I remember her wanting to help the elderly, so she placed an ad in the newspaper offering free cleaning services. She received a lot of interest, and I went along with her while she cleaned. She explained to me that she just wanted to help, even in small ways.

It took me years to understand this side of my mother. Mom had difficulty holding a regular job, but she was fully capable of showing care and compassion. I didn't completely grasp how her childhood experiences had shaped her. She told me bits of stories over time, but it wasn't until later that I realized their profound impact on her life. Those experiences had left her unable to function in the way society typically expected.

My earliest memories of Mom were of an active and caring single mother. As I grew into my teens, however, our relationship changed. Although we grew apart in adulthood, I now recognize similarities between us. Mom had a darker, moodier side that I didn't fully understand until later. I eventually learned that she struggled with depression. She drank and had on-and-off relationships, which also shaped our family dynamic.

As a youth, I started doing small acts of kindness with friends, inspired by Mom. Later, as an adult, I made more deliberate plans to incorporate these values into my life purpose

I also inherited Mom's sense of cooking—not to the level Mom used to cook, but well enough to provide for my own family. Her example of making the best of what we had during my younger years stayed with me, even though we didn't have a close relationship later in life.

Dad, on the other hand, lived most of his life in Bearskin Lake, a small community located south of the James Bay region. He came from a large family with many siblings, four brothers and four sisters.

Some of my earliest memories of Dad go back to when my parents were still together. I remember him bringing us a cat in the middle of winter. I don't know where he got it, but it arrived in a crate and looked half frozen. Back then, we travelled to and from town by snowmobile, and by sled for groceries and rides to school. As young as I was, I still remember riding on the back of a sled in the winter, likely on my way to daycare. The house was heated by a woodstove, which was typical for that area.

After my parents separated, I lost contact with Dad and my brother for a few years. There were occasional visits when they came to Thunder Bay, but I remember missing them both and feeling like the visits were too infrequent.

Dad was a quiet person but also very intelligent. I remember he always worked in the band office doing administrative tasks. He handled accounting, served as a band councillor, managed fuel supplies, and worked on various town projects.

He wasn't around very often in my childhood years, so I don't have many memories of being together during that time. It wasn't until I was a preteen that I went to visit Dad and his family for Christmas. That was a nice experience because my grandparents lived in a house next door to Dad's and many of my cousins had homes within walking distance. Visiting them was easy, and it felt like I was part of a close-knit community.

I remember the time Dad taught me how to snare rabbits. We took the snowmobile out to a quiet area, and he taught me how to set up a small snare. When we returned later to check it, I was surprised to find we had caught a rabbit. It was my first one. Dad asked me to hold it up for a photo, but I remember feeling conflicted because I still thought of rabbits as pets. At home with Mom, I had a pet rabbit, so I wasn't smiling in that photo.

That moment highlighted the differences between my life in the city and life in the North with Dad. Life up North was much more connected to the land and wildlife. We often had fish, moose, or duck for dinner at my grandparents' home, and Grandma would make homemade bannock and hearty soups.

Neither of my grandparents spoke English, so I eventually learned some Oji-Cree to communicate with them. Some of my favourite things to say were "Atteh puhki shooniyaa?" which meant, "Can I get some money?" and "Atteh, odaaban nowiyabichdoon?" which meant, "Can I borrow the snowmobile?" Usually, they would respond with "eha" or "ow," meaning "yes."

Their home reflected their deep Christian faith. I remember the walls were adorned with religious pictures, including a prominent one of the Last Supper. They had a strong faith and prayed together every morning and evening. That is one of my clearest memories of them as a couple.

Sometimes I spent the night at their home. They would wake up at 6 a.m. to pray and read aloud from their Cree and syllabic books from the Anglican Church. I didn't know much about Christianity at the time, but I recognized the Anglican connection from examining their books out of curiosity. It wasn't until college that I began to understand the history of the Oji-Cree and Cree and their connection to faith and culture.

My grandpa passed on a few years later while living under my aunt's care, but I was happy he got to meet my husband and son before his passing. Both my grandparents are buried in a small cemetery on the south side of Bearskin Lake, the place they lived for most of their lives.

When I asked Dad whether my grandparents had shared any stories before they passed, he told me about Grandma's brother Vernon, who would be my great-uncle. He'd travelled with the Bay when he was nineteen years old—in the early 1900s, back when workers used York boats to cross through water passageways. In the northern Ontario region, the main passageway was the Severn River. This was historically how the

Hudson Bay Company transported its many goods inland. But my Kookum's brother was young and had an accident during one of these ventures. The northern waters can be rough and full of slippery rocks. Vernon fell in the rapids during one of the river runs and passed away. He was buried somewhere along the Severn River.

Chapter 2
TEEN YEARS

When I was a preteen, Mom sent me to Bearskin Lake to live and attend school. During these years, I began to struggle with studying. I also grappled with my relationship with my parents. By the time I was a teen, my relationship with Mom had grown distant—not just because of the physical distance between us but because, once I moved, I rarely heard from her.

I began experimenting with common street drugs and also took up smoking in an attempt to fit in. I was pretty awkward—I had braces and wore contact lenses, which eventually froze in the harsh winter. I struggled with self-confidence and often stayed out late with friends. Some nights we snowmobiled around town, dragging a sled tied to the back. It was reckless, and we often got into trouble for it. Other nights we'd hang out in town, sitting under the stars until one of us got access to a four-wheeler we could drive around.

I often felt an inexplicable loneliness when I was home alone at night. I began searching for God and pondering the meaning of life. Besides watching my grandparents pray and attending the occasional Anglican church service, I hadn't had much guidance or direction in my spiritual journey.

One winter evening, there was a special service at the community's Full Gospel Church. An evangelical preacher was visiting, and his ministry was dedicated to youth. At the time, many young people attended these services and gave their lives to Christ. I went with friends—Joyce, Amanda, Tiffany, and Sophia—and we didn't plan to stay long. We were just curious about the speaker. However, the service took an unexpected turn, and before we knew it, all of us were standing at the front, ready to give our lives to Christ. I remember spending most of that night crying and so did my friends. When I returned home, I didn't realize it immediately, but something within me had started to change.

A Bible verse that meant a lot to me was, *"Therefore, if anyone is in Christ, the new creation has come: The old has gone, the new is here!"* (2 Corinthians 5:17) I understood its meaning—I felt the change in my heart and was truly happy.

I moved to Sault Ste. Marie for ninth grade and lived with Mom again. We were in a cozy two-bedroom unit above a hair salon, a rental she shared with her common-law boyfriend. At the time, I didn't think much of it, as long as we could manage our day-to-day routines. Mom knew I was a Christian, though she herself wasn't a believer. Occasionally, she attended First Baptist Church down the street and I joined her. That's how I got involved in the church youth group, which marked a turning point in my Christian walk.

Initially, I was quiet and shy during church activities. I attended weekly high school Bible studies and developed a few innocent crushes on boys at church. Things changed when our youth leader organized a trip to the U.S. for a conference called "Acquire the Fire." There was some fundraising involved, but the youth pastor later called to say an anonymous donor had covered my expenses. I was thrilled and ready to go.

The conference was an amazing experience, and I made new friends along the way. Things really changed, though, when I signed up for a youth missions group based in Fort Worth, Texas. My faith was challenged and strengthened by the Bible verse, "*He said to them, 'Go into all the world and preach the gospel to all creation'*" (Mark 16:15).

Our mission group was set to leave in a few weeks, but I needed to raise the funds for the trip. The conference team challenged me to trust God and have faith that He would provide. I didn't even know my exact destination at first, as teams were heading to various countries. Ultimately, I chose South Africa.

I raised funds by sending out letters and sharing a short testimony in church. I also applied for a passport, and within a few short weeks, God had provided everything I needed, right down to the luggage and small travel items for Africa. I remember the team sending out a specific packing list, emphasizing that we only bring the basics. First, we went to Fort Worth for training, a time of intense heat that flew by quickly while we were taught through drama-based stories. Then the teams were sent off to various locations in Africa.

Our group consisted of about twenty teens and two leaders. We embarked on the trip to South Africa and stayed on church grounds in Johannesburg, perched on a hill with breathtaking scenery.

Toward the end of the four-week trip, our team spent a week in Mozambique. We lived in grass huts and slept on the ground with only our sleeping bags. The showers were rudimentary—just a bowl of water that we used to wash and rinse ourselves. We were strictly instructed not to wander outside at night due to hyenas and other such dangers.

We stayed in an area that was part of an orphanage. During the day, we played with the children and visited various communities. The groups we met were always excited to see us, and the experience was profoundly eye-opening.

I vividly recall the woman who ran the orphanage. Her name was Carol, and she shared her testimony with us. Carol had left her ordinary life in the States to live in Mozambique indefinitely, trusting God to provide for the orphanage, even though she managed it alone.

She asked us a question that stayed with me: "What is your calling?" Her words resonated deeply, and I began to reflect on my own life. Was God calling me to become a missionary? Was I willing to give up everything to devote my life to ministry? How would that look? These questions swirled in my mind.

Despite the uncertainty, I felt incredibly close to God. Each morning, we prayed. I cherished those moments of connection with Him—watching the sun rise over Mozambique, my hair done up in messy braids that had been lovingly crafted by the children.

Carol shared stories about challenges the orphanage had faced. She urged us to keep the children in our prayers and gave everyone a T-shirt to remember them by. Mine was golden-yellow and had the words *Pray for the children of Mozambique* printed on it. I often wore it back home in Canada. I brought back photos I had taken during the trip—pictures of the kids, the breathtaking landscapes, and the various locations we'd visited, including Swaziland. In Swaziland, I bought a beautiful candle set, some intricately carved wooden giraffes, and a vibrant purple skirt with unique dye patterns.

I knew I was destined to be a missionary, and the confirmation came during my flight home. I'd been seated next to a Christian doctor who somehow recognized I was a Christian as well—perhaps I was reading something from the trip, though I don't quite remember. He shared that he was on his way to do ministry in China. I told him that I, too, wanted to go to China, and at that moment, I felt a clear calling that my next mission trip would take me there.

At the time, I didn't have a solid plan for travelling to China. It was a closed country, which meant I couldn't join a ministry group as I had done for South Africa. In addition, I was still in high school with another year or so until graduation.

To gain a better understanding of life in China and the type of work I might do there, I began searching for volunteer opportunities. Through a connection at my church—First Baptist Church in Sault Ste. Marie—I met Cynthia, who had recently returned from a ministry trip to China. She told me about an American couple she'd met during her travels, and they gave me a contact for a volunteer internship opportunity with a company in China.

I applied and went through the process of getting my visa to work abroad voluntarily. After my graduation from high school, I worked for the company in China, and that is how I was introduced to Matthew, our supervisor. Originally from Texas, Matthew was tall and friendly, and we quickly connected over shared experiences. He, too, had moved away from home to do this work in China. He even knew about the ministry I had worked with during my trip to South Africa.

The company was located in a small town on the outskirts of Beijing, which was about a forty-five-minute drive away. There was a nice two-storey building with a few suites on the second level. I was provided with a room that had two bunk beds, a bathroom, and a small kitchen. I felt completely lost at first. The grocery shopping was so different there that I barely used the kitchen— mostly I ate from the kitchen provided for the factory workers.

For two months, I worked as a daily cleaner and caretaker at the orphanage. During the last four weeks, I was a factory worker and an English teacher. Each day I would go through the strollers to sweep them out, then tidy up the toys and sometimes wash them. I also wiped down the cribs and refilled the baby wipes, diapers, and formula. Although I wasn't supposed to spend too much time with the babies, I always snuck in some playtime with them.

One little boy named Daniel was especially adorable. I considered myself lucky because I took him for walks on the days his usual caretaker was away. I was also in charge of his feeding and sleeping schedules during the day. In the evening, another nanny would come in. That part of my stay made the entire trip to China worthwhile.

In China, I made a few friends from the States and also spent time visiting the couple who ran the orphanage. They were both doctors from Australia and had used their own funds to build the orphanage. They were truly devoted to the mission. I spent some evenings there, enjoying meals with them and learning more about their lives and work. They even told me the story of how they adopted a little girl while also running the orphanage. I felt fortunate to meet a group of Christian believers who were willing to leave the comforts of home and relocate to China to do this work.

The gospel was spreading in that small community. Although my journey was quite solitary much of the time, I never felt alone because of the strong sense of community I became a part of there.

Sara was a young student I met there, a German science major. We decided to take a trip to Shanghai together and then continue on to Xi'an by train. It was a long trip, and we didn't speak any Mandarin. However, it turned out to be a memorable experience. We got by using our dictionaries and took photos whenever we could. Sara and I got along really well, despite the tiring journey.

In Shanghai, we stayed in a youth hostel. It was located in an older hotel, and the floors creaked when you walked down the hall. We also noticed the sound of rats in the walls, which creeped us out a little—we worried the rats might get into our bags. On the upside, we discovered there was a movie being filmed in the corridor!

I loved the scenery in Shanghai. The contrast between the modern and ancient parts of the city was striking. As we wandered through an old market, we bought some lovely souvenirs. We did the same in Xi'an. I remember buying a back scratcher for my dad because he always needs one.

Xi'an was an interesting place to visit. Our tour was conducted entirely in Mandarin, so we missed the stories and history; however, we stopped at several amazing locations. My favourite spot was the Terracotta Warriors and the surrounding market.

My purpose on this trip was to discover where God wanted me to work in the future. I hoped to return home and find work in that field. For the most part, I wasn't aiming to become a doctor or spend my savings building an orphanage like the couple I'd met in China. So working in an orphanage wasn't something I seriously considered for my future.

What I truly enjoyed was teaching English in my evening class. I taught the children the alphabet and some words that corresponded to each letter. Teaching English was new to me, and I hadn't considered it as a profession before. But the kids were so much fun and were enthusiastic about learning. The class was packed each week, with the parents sitting quietly in the back. Our lessons were simple, primarily focused on word repetition. Through this experience, I decided I would return to China as an ESL teacher.

Chapter 3
COLLEGE YEARS

After returning to Canada, I spent a year deciding where to study. I was looking for teaching programs specifically related to teaching English. I explored various colleges and universities and even considered pursuing a Bachelor of Education but changed my mind because I wanted a college that had a Christian theological background.

After researching Bible colleges across Canada—focusing on programs that offered teaching opportunities—I finally decided to attend Providence College in Otterburne, Manitoba. It is now called Providence University College. Their TESOL program (Teaching English to Speakers of Other Languages) is offered as a one-year ESL teaching certificate, and I believed it would be useful for teaching abroad. As far as the degree I would pursue, I eventually decided on a Bachelor of Arts in Social Sciences during my first year of study.

Providence is a small university college located in rural Manitoba and surrounded by farmland. Originally called Winnipeg Bible Training School, Providence was founded in 1925 and has changed its name a few times over the years. When I first arrived, I was surprised at how far it was from the city of Winnipeg—about a forty-five-minute drive. I'd heard stories about its isolation and soon found out for myself that, unless you owned a vehicle, it could be challenging to find a ride. The campus featured a large old bell tower, two student dormitories, and later, a newly constructed cafeteria.

My first year at Providence was probably the most memorable. Initially, I was a bit uncertain of what to expect, but the welcome event for new students soon allowed me to make some new friends. I met a group of colleagues from Ontario who wanted to study and pursue a Christian education, just as I did. My classmates shared goals and beliefs similar to mine. College was a turning point for me. Until then, I'd spent most of my high school years and home life in a non-Christian environment. I'd had close friends in high school, attended a youth group, and even lived with my youth pastor's family for a time, yet I didn't realize the sense of loneliness I'd carried until I found the community at Providence.

I enrolled in the TESOL certificate program because I felt God was guiding me to teach English as a missionary in China. What I couldn't have predicted was how much Providence would offer me beyond that teacher training. I made friends who shared my faith and even knew my hometown area well. It felt like a genuine community. Altogether, I spent three years at Providence, and those years shaped me significantly.

In the beginning, I often thought about the fact that Providence was a smaller college—not particularly well-known or recognized for its academic reputation. However, in my heart,

I trusted God to provide for my future, and in many ways, He did, despite these concerns.

When I first began my studies, I'd imagined myself teaching children like those I'd met in China. Things didn't turn out that way. My first real experience as an ESL instructor came during my practicum, and for this, we were required to find a teaching placement. Clueless as to how to go about it, I sent a request to a nearby university in Winnipeg. Thankfully, they were familiar with Providence's ESL program, so it wasn't difficult to get accepted.

I was incredibly nervous about my first practicum. I'd never taught university-level students—it was a world apart from working with kids. If you'd seen me that first day, I probably looked like a deer in the headlights. Still, I put on a brave face, dressed in what I thought was "appropriate teaching attire"—dress pants and a nice blouse—and headed off. I arrived with a couple classmates who were also completing their practicums there.

To be honest, I wish I'd kept my first lesson plan. It would be interesting to look back and see how much my teaching style has changed since that day. (If I recall correctly, the lesson might have been based on the lyrics of an Avril Lavigne song!) Whatever it was, I now know it wasn't the best way to start a class or make a good first impression. The students were not fans of my class.

Initially, we had a nice group of five students, most of whom were Chinese Mandarin speakers. They were friendly, and I was especially glad to have a few girls in the group—I thought maybe I could relate to them better. But after that first lesson, attendance dropped dramatically. By the end of the practicum, I was down to one male student. Thankfully, he didn't seem to mind my music-based lesson plan.

Chapter 4
LIFE IN CHINA

By graduation time, I knew I would teach abroad, despite my early struggles with building lesson plans. I reached out to some friends for advice on where to apply. My friend Roy was from mainland China, and he contacted his former university on my behalf. Thanks to him, I received a contract offer from Changchun University of Technology shortly after graduation.

After packing up from college, I stayed with my brother and his family while preparing to leave for China. Changchun is in the northeastern region of China, in the province of Jilin. The city is best known for its Puppet Manchurian Palace Museum. If you've seen the 1987 movie *The Last Emperor,* you might recognize this as Emperor Pu Yi's residence. The palace is now a museum, offering a glimpse into the rich history of the area.

Once in Changchun, I prepared myself for teaching university students again. This time, my classes were much larger—over thirty students per class, though I can't recall the exact headcount. It was definitely overwhelming at first.

I had a good group of students and especially enjoyed teaching my writing class, for which I relied on a textbook kindly lent to me by a Canadian coworker. My courses included business writing, English conversation or speaking, and business English. My income wasn't very high compared to Canadian standards, but it was enough to live comfortably in China. I remember calculating my salary in Canadian dollars—it was about three hundred dollars per month.

My coworkers included two Americans, Carrie and Janet; two Filipino teachers, Mac and Millie; one British teacher named Aaron; a Scottish teacher named Nick; and one other Canadian, Doug. Aaron took me around town to introduce me to local restaurants and shopping areas. My favourite places to shop were Guilin Lu and Chongqing Lu.

It wasn't until the winter holiday that I travelled to South Korea on my own for some sightseeing. I stayed with Ashley, a former Providence classmate who had completed the same program. I slept on her floor for a couple weeks, and since she worked, I spent most of my days exploring Seoul on my own.

I visited all the major shopping districts in the city. In one shop, I picked up a ceramic figurine of a Korean couple, which later became a gift for a college friend. I also bought a small Korean Bible, thinking I would gift it to one of my students back in Changchun. For myself, I purchased soaps from Lush and a green hooded sweatshirt with a teddy bear design.

The rest of my holiday was spent travelling to central China with my coworker Carrie. We visited Xi'an by train and were accompanied by her student Vivial, who studied tourism and acted as our personal guide. This was my second visit to the Terracotta Warriors, but the experience remained awe-inspiring. We also visited Ba Xian An, or the Temple of the Eight Immortals, which is located in the mountains. I bought a shadow puppet as a souvenir during this trip.

One of the highlights was a hike on Mount Li, where we took a picture in front of large Chinese characters carved into the stone. This location holds historical significance for Xi'an and is known as Bingjian Ting, or the Remonstrance Pavilion. Aside from sightseeing, Vivial took us souvenir shopping and also introduced us to the local restaurants, where we enjoyed some of Xi'an's renowned delicacies. One of my favourites was the Roujia-mo—also known as a Chinese hamburger—which is pork served in pita bread. Another Xi'an specialty is their dumplings.

Back in Changchun, I became close to a few students, one of whom was a Korean Chinese girl named Kate. She came to visit me in the apartment provided by the university, and I slipped her a gift as she left for the student dormitory. I continued to keep in touch with Kate, and later when she moved to Dalian, I visited her for a day. To this day, I still receive emails from her and am reminded of the friendliness of those students. I miss the communications from them, and Kate is one of the few students I've managed to keep in touch with throughout the years.

I slowly got to know a few of the other Changchun teachers, aside from my own coworkers. I joined an international fellowship and attended their services every Sunday. It wasn't a very large group, but I made some friends there.

In late spring, once the holiday was over, I attended a birthday event being held among the expats. The restaurant was packed, and people filled every table in the room. I sat with another teacher, and when I got up to grab a drink, I was introduced to a couple named Andy and Monica. The introductions were brief, but I still remember Andy's face when he learned I was Canadian. He seemed curious about my ethnicity, so I told him I was Indigenous. His eyes filled with surprise. He said something like, "Wow, I've never met anyone who is Canadian Indigenous." Andy was British Russian, and Monica was from the Philippines. We exchanged numbers.

As I continued to meet more teachers in Changchun, I encountered an Aussie guy named Sean, and we messaged for a while. I liked him at the time and wanted to get to know him better. I found out that he'd worked in Changchun for a few years and had taught in the local primary schools. Other than that, my social life consisted of various meeting invites as I became more familiar with life among the local expats.

One day I received an invitation for coffee from Andy and Monica. I thought it was a bit odd for a couple to send out an invite, but I agreed. A while later, they broke up, though I didn't know the reason at the time. Eventually, I met up with Andy and a coworker named Michelle, and we hung out at a local cafe.

I became close friends with Michelle, who was pretty funny. We had a good time whenever we went out for dinner or coffee. Soon after, I noticed that Andy had started tagging along with us. Andy worked at a primary school, and I was surprised at how small (and cute) his students were. Some of them were in kindergarten. He worked for a local company called Tian

Shua, which hired teachers and sent them to various schools in the area, even outside the city. Andy had been a professional writer before becoming a teacher and decided to join one of the English Corners I held for my students in the park. He was the same age as me, and I eventually let him convince me to go out for coffee.

Soon the year had ended, and everyone departed. I didn't receive a contract renewal from Changchun University due to program changes in the English department. Despite this change, my employer had arranged for a new employer to hire me for the fall term and paid for a return ticket to Canada.

I returned for a second year in Changchun after a short summer break. I'd worked as a dishwasher in a gold mine during those summer months. My boss didn't mind that I was only working for a few weeks, and he used to tell me about his marriage to a Chinese woman. I found this interesting and listened carefully as he explained more about the visa process. His help would eventually guide some of my decisions later on in life.

During my second year, I taught a few conversational class-es, and overall, I found the fall term to be more challenging in my second year. I was still trying out new lessons and topics in class. Seeing as I didn't have the textbooks preferred by the college, I had to come up with my own lesson plans. Sometimes they were well received, but other times, not so much.

I'd stayed in touch with Andy during the summer months, and as soon as I was back in Changchun, we decided to start dating. We spent time getting to know each other better. I asked him how he'd ended up in an unlikely place like Changchun and discovered that he'd travelled because he was a writer. Andy grew up speaking Russian and studied English in school, but aside from English as a second language, he also spoke fluent Uzbek and German. He'd studied English as part of his bachelor's degree and worked as a translator for an international nonprofit organization. Not only was he well educated, but he was in China for more than just the "experience." When you spend time in China, you tend to meet teachers with different plans or purposes for being there. Andy's goals were to teach and find topics to write about, and that was something I liked about him.

He taught me some important things, such as focusing more on my physical health while I was in China. This was an area I'd struggled with my first year. My grocery shopping was almost nonexistent, and I wasn't sure which meals to prepare for myself—I mostly cooked rice, eggs, and vegetables. Andy taught me how to make homemade soups, both beef and chicken noodle.

After six months, we decided to pursue a more committed relationship. As I considered Andy as a long-term partner, one thing that was important to me was his openness to becoming a believer in Christ. He always joined me at the international church in Changchun, and we got to know the members there pretty well. Andy and I were grateful to have found a second family apart from our own while living abroad. We got married in a small rural church just outside of Changchun on June 16, 2007.

We chose to marry in China because, during the planning, I realized that marrying in Canada would involve a long wait to acquire a visa. I learned this from my previous employer, who'd gone through the same process with his Chinese wife. It's easier to marry abroad than to wait for a visa. That's how we ended up marrying outside our home countries, so far away from our families.

Andy's mother flew into China to join the wedding, and I had a childhood friend come in as my bridesmaid. Andy's mom gave us some Russian heirlooms, which I thought was very special. Growing up, I had never been given jewellery, let alone family heirlooms. She gave us two beautiful rings—one with flower designs and another with a large diamond—and a chain necklace. When she gifted us these treasures, she spoke a Russian saying over us: "Every wife should have a necklace." I've worn the chain necklace every day since.

For our honeymoon, we waited until winter break. In China, winter break is two months long. We spent that time in Thailand, on Koh Chang Island and Koh Mak Island. Before heading to the islands, however, we passed a few days in Bangkok, exploring the local markets and trying out small cafes. We also visited the Grand Palace, which has golden rooftops—it's a beautiful place to visit.

It's a full day of travel from Bangkok to Koh Chang Island, but overall, the journey was fairly comfortable and not overly crowded—quite a relief after living in China where public transport is almost always jam-packed.

When we first arrived on the island, we didn't have a room booked in advance. We watched as our bus dropped off other tourists at their hotels and decided to simply jump off at a random stop and book a room. We slept in a small cabin at that hotel, and it was dark by the time we unpacked. As we were settling down for the night, I noticed a huge gecko climbing on the ceiling above us. It was the first time I'd ever seen a gecko, and I was too scared to try to catch it. I barely slept that night.

The next morning, we walked around to see what else was available and found a place nearby called JB Resort. It had charming log cabins close to the beach. For one month, we could literally step out of the cabin and walk twenty feet before finding ourselves on the beach. It was beautiful. Everything about the island felt so peaceful. Our section of the island was fairly quiet, with the larger resorts located farther north on the popular White Sands Beach. My favourite part of our stay was the evening beach walks, where we could stop at resort bars along the way and order cocktails. To be honest, I haven't had cocktails anywhere that compare to the ones served in Thailand. The locals who ran most of the services were incredibly friendly.

That's where we spent our first month. We tried everything we could, including hiking, kayaking, snorkelling, and elephant rides. The Thai food was amazing, too. My favourite dish was Massaman curry, although all the food was simply delicious.

The day we went snorkelling, we took a small boat out into the ocean to explore nearby islands. I remember swimming behind the tour guide as he pointed out various sea creatures on the ocean floor. I saw sea urchins, which were fascinating but also a little intimidating. The moment I started feeling really nervous was when the guide mentioned the sharks nearby. Although they were small sharks, I couldn't help but feel uneasy.

For the second month, we decided to visit the island of Koh Mak. We travelled there by boat and spent the remainder of our time in Thailand exploring its beauty. During this time, we stayed in a small bungalow and hiked the trails, discovering new parts of the island. The islands have changed a lot since then. The resort we stayed at in Koh Mak was modest at the time, with a small dining area on a deck with just a couple tables next to the beach. Now it has expanded into a beautiful resort with a larger, open sitting area, and the bungalows have been upgraded. When we were there, Koh Mak had just a handful of resorts, and we spent most of our time in a small bungalow on the far end of the island. We ate at the resort but also tried some local roadside dining, which offered simple yet delicious meals.

Koh Mak is home to some of the most beautiful and pristine beaches in the world. We did a bike tour of the island that took us through lush jungle paths and led to private beaches. I remember cycling for a couple hours with only a bottle of water to sustain me. When we finally reached the beach, I sat and gulped down the water, feeling completely exhausted but fulfilled. Along the bike trail, there were signs telling stories about the lost turtles that had once populated the island. Time stood still there. For two months, we enjoyed Thai food and the company of other tourists.

One thing Andy didn't know was that the summer before we got married, while I was back in Canada for the break, I had attended a church for the first time and had an interesting experience there. During my visit to this small fellowship in Thunder Bay, I met a pastor, and without knowing who I was, he approached me and began to prophesy. He saw me walking on a beach, peaceful and surrounded by clear water. He told me that God was going to bless me for being obedient. That day on Koh Mak Island, after cycling through the jungle and landing sweaty and satisfied on the beach, I truly felt like God's promise was with us. That peaceful moment on the beach seemed to bring the pastor's vision to life.

My third year of teaching was highly challenging, and yet I found it the most fulfilling. I had decided to switch employers, and Andy's employer convinced me to work for them. I wasn't overly confident about the change but was willing to give it a try. Although I'd done small stints teaching high school before, this was a full-time position with elementary school children.

Transitioning from the university level to working with young children wasn't easy. Some teachers are naturally dynamic and thrive in front of a class full of kids, especially the large classrooms typical of Chinese schools. For me, it was a struggle. The school, however, offered a generous allowance to hire both Andy and me for a few months, and this made the opportunity worth exploring.

While Andy was naturally energetic and great with children, I found it hard to muster that kind of energy at 8 a.m. (And don't get me started on the prospect of dancing and singing with the kids at that time of day.) By the end of the term, I don't think the school was interested in renewing my contract—and honestly, I didn't mind. Teaching young children just wasn't my calling.

That said, a major upside of the experience was that we were able to save most of our earnings from that time. This financial cushion ultimately helped us make the move to Canada.

In the meantime, I returned to teaching university students, and to be honest, it became the highlight of my teaching career. I was hired by Northeast Normal University, one of the best universities in Changchun, to teach in a business program affiliated with an Australian university. From the moment I met my program manager, we got along well, and I felt fortunate to be part of such a reputable institution. In hindsight, I wish I had spent all three years teaching there; it was truly the ideal environment for me.

I was impressed with my students, who were motivated and hardworking, as well as my coworkers—both the English teachers and local faculty. Among the other English teachers, there was Frank (an American), Tyler (a British professor), and Dan (a Canadian). I had met them previously at social gatherings where expat teachers would bond over drinks and food, sharing stories about life in China.

Frank was a good friend of Andy's, and we even planned a weekend trip together to the seaside city of Qingdao. It was a refreshing getaway, sightseeing in a coastal city and sampling new foods and drinks from the area. Tyler impressed me with his dedication and experience. He split his time between the UK and China, working in each country for six months at a time. While he never mentioned it outright, we all knew he was a seasoned professor from a top British university. Dan was the most talkative in our group, sharing countless stories about his adventures and challenges in China.

Despite the many positives, there was a downside to my situation—one that lingered and affected how I was perceived by others. The reality of standing in front of a classroom was that I "looked Chinese." This often led to confusion among the students. If I was Canadian, why didn't I have blonde hair or blue eyes? The unspoken assumption that all Canadians fit a specific image was difficult to overcome.

This preconception also influenced how some of my fellow expats perceived Andy and me. It became part of my experience living and working in China. I was constantly told that I looked Chinese, and after a while, it became tiresome. I could sense my students' initial disappointment that I didn't match their expectations of what a foreign teacher should look like. With employers, the differences were even more apparent. For instance, my second-year employer would occasionally drop off gifts for the teachers, but some of us were excluded. The favoritism was obvious. I wasn't the tall American with blonde hair and blue eyes—I was Canadian, but I didn't "look the part."

These moments often made me question what I was doing there. At times, I felt inadequate and out of place. But deep down, I knew God had a purpose for me in China. Even though I didn't always understand what it was or whether I was making a meaningful impact, I believed I was there because I was meant to be.

Despite the challenges, my last term at Northeast Normal University turned out to be the most enjoyable and fulfilling. My students were engaged and enthusiastic, and many told me they would never forget the time we spent together. I felt the same way. For the first time, I had a group of students performing well in English at the academic level required for studying abroad. This was a significant contrast to previous classes, where it was often a struggle to get students to form sentences, let alone perform academically in English.

During that final term, I introduced critical thinking projects, and the students worked on presentations and group activities. It turned out to be a highly rewarding experience for all of us.

Meanwhile, Andy and I spent the year saving money and working on his permanent residence visa for Canada. From the time we submitted the application at the embassy in Beijing, it took about six months for him to receive approval. When the term ended, I returned to Canada and began preparing for the next chapter of our lives together.

Part 2
SPRING/SĪKWAN

Chapter 5
RETURNING TO CANADA

My departure from China was exhausting; I left with so many thoughts weighing on my mind. But I was thankful for the friendly faces that greeted me when I returned to Canada. Three of my college friends met me at the airport and helped carry my bags. I remember we couldn't stop laughing because Joyce, who had a broken leg in a cast, somehow ended up pushing all my baggage.

We went out for dinner at Perkins and caught up on travel news and life changes. A significant shift had taken place—I had returned as a married woman. Interestingly, my friend Pam, a former dorm mate, had also recently married someone from college. Transitioning back to life in Canada wasn't easy, and I was so grateful that my friends didn't forget about me during this period.

When I look back at our transition to life in Canada, I feel like we could have planned it better. Initially, Andy and I had intended to pursue master's degrees, aiming to advance our careers. We'd planned to move to Winnipeg and apply to universities there—I was considering a master's in counselling psychology, while Andy wanted to pursue a degree in communications. Both of us applied to Providence University College and were accepted. I was set to start in the fall, with Andy planning for the following term once he'd received his visa. Ultimately, however, the timing didn't quite turn out that way.

I had a couple months to find a rental. Andy and I needed at least a one-bedroom apartment. I stayed with a few different friends while I sorted everything out and then settled into a small older basement unit to wait for Andy's visa and continue searching for a place. During this time, I found out I was pregnant. Surprisingly, I hadn't experienced any morning sickness or noticeable symptoms, so between all the travel and the adjustment to life in Canada, it hadn't crossed my mind.

Eventually, I found a small basement apartment in an older building and arranged to commute from Winnipeg to Otterburne for my college courses. But after starting my first few counselling classes, I began to question whether counselling psychology was the right path for me. I'd always thought it would be, considering my background in social sciences. It seemed like a natural choice, but I soon realized it might not be the best fit.

By second term, I decided to withdraw before my grades suffered. I told myself I could revisit my study plans after the baby arrived. Despite this decision, I enjoyed my time at the college. It helped me reconnect with old friends and kept my mind occupied while waiting for Andy to arrive in Canada. That waiting period was perhaps the hardest part. Uncertainty loomed. Would the government approve his visa in time?

Would I have to give birth alone? How long could I manage on my own? These questions often played in the back of my mind.

During this time, Andy's mom sent over some thoughtful baby gifts—tiny newborn outfits, adorable onesies with mitts, and soft baby bonnets. She sent so much, and it touched me that she was thinking of the baby from so far away. My own mom lived much closer, in Thunder Bay, and was just an eight-hour drive away—yet she didn't send anything for the baby.

Thankfully, Andy's visa came through as expected after a six-month wait. He was granted permanent residence, which allowed him to work and live in Canada. He arrived in the middle of winter, during one of Winnipeg's coldest months—early January. My dad was visiting for the Christmas holidays, and he accompanied me to the airport to meet Andy. By then, I already had a noticeable baby bump. It was Andy's first time meeting my dad, and I was so grateful to have both of them close by.

Shortly after Andy arrived in Winnipeg, we began searching for work opportunities for him. He started by volunteering at a local newspaper organization, where he got to meet many of my old coworkers. It wasn't long before he'd secured part-time work as a telephone marketer at a small research office.

With his salary, we managed to make ends meet, and living expenses weren't too difficult to handle. The timing worked out well, as it gave us some breathing room to prepare for the baby's arrival.

Chapter 6
A GROWING FAMILY

The temperatures were still cold when we took the bus to the Women's Hospital. I'd decided to check in when I started having contractions.

The next morning, March 20, 2009, our baby arrived. He was a big boy, weighing nine pounds. I remember he cried at first, but the nurse wrapped him in a small blanket, and he quieted down almost immediately. I spent a couple days recovering at the hospital, though I barely slept. Joyce came in to visit, and soon enough, we took our son, Alistaire Darling, home by taxi, bundled up in a baby carrier with a soft blanket covering him.

Andy chose the name Alistaire because he liked British names, and honestly, I loved it, too. It reminded me of a character from a British novel. Alistaire means "defender of the people" and has Scottish or Greek origins.

It felt like the perfect time for him to join us—the snow was melting, and when the weather warmed up, I could take him out for walks. I remember a bunny often sat outside our living room window, and it always made me think of Alistaire because he was my spring baby.

We had started attending a nondenominational church downtown. I liked it because it was close to the heart of the city, and people often came in off the street. It was a short bus ride for us, so we decided to join the church fellowship and attend regularly.

In a short time, we made many new friends. I joined a women's group, mostly young moms, and soon after we got home with Alistaire, I didn't have to worry about making meals. The ladies from the church group came over and brought homemade meals for the first week—taco soup, broth, lo mein noodles, bread, and more.

Joyce, who was part of the same church, organized a baby shower for us there. I remember the beautiful setup of various foods. We enjoyed snacks, chatted, and had the chance to meet other young couples who attended the shower. It was such a blessing, and Alistaire received so many clothes and blankets that he had everything he needed. I recall barely having to buy a thing that first year because he had enough outfits for each month.

My mom decided to visit us for a couple weeks. She gave Alistaire a little baby outfit: a pair of jeans and a nice collared white top, kind of a preppy style, along with little sandals. It was good to have her visit us, and it was one of the few times she made the effort to be near Alistaire. After two weeks, she left and returned to Thunder Bay.

My dad knew someone who made baby wraps called Tukobisin in Oji-Cree. The wrap was handmade from material with a zigzag pattern in orange, tan, and black. It's a traditional way for mothers to carry their babies, and surprisingly, Alistaire really liked it. I think the Tukobisin kept him warm in our chilly basement.

Andy and I used to enjoy taking walks in the summer. We lived in a quiet neighbourhood close to downtown, which was still safe enough for us to stroll to the park. Baby Alistaire was adorable, and he always got a lot of attention. His face looked just like Andy's, though he had dark-brown hair and eyes. He always had big eyes, which he still has now as he's grown older. Overall, he was a happy baby. As soon as someone picked him up, he would flash a huge smile, and even on walks, he was joyful. I remember taking him to a small corner baby shop where the cashier commented that she hoped to have a baby as happy as Alistaire was. I didn't realize how lucky I was—we had all the typical baby challenges, but overall, I think he was fairly easy to care for.

Chapter 7
WORK AND LIFE

A year and a half later, Andy transitioned into stable work as a program manager for a diabetes-focused Indigenous organization. Not only did the job provide security, but Andy also really enjoyed his work. With that in place, we started looking for a new home.

Our search began in Winnipeg, where we looked at older homes in the South Saint Vital area. I soon realized, however, that our budget might not allow us to buy within the city limits. After some searching, we found a small two-bedroom house with a large yard outside the city. We liked it enough to make an offer, and it was accepted.

Shortly after receiving the good news, the three of us drove to Banff, Alberta, for a long spring break trip. Although the road trip was tiring, it was refreshing to get away and visit beautiful Banff. It was our first time there—I had visited Alberta in my younger years, but I'd never made it to Banff. Known for its breathtaking Rocky Mountain views, it was the perfect getaway. By this time, Alistaire was two years old and walking on his own.

We took the Banff gondola ride up to the top of Sulphur Mountain, and I remember Alistaire's ear-to-ear smile as we ascended. The view from the top was absolutely amazing. We walked along the visitors' trail, complete with fenced-in viewing poles and steps—steps, steps, and more steps. We stopped often to take photos together, soaking in the beauty of the place.

Once again, we felt blessed as a family. Andy and I celebrated our small "house victory" by going out for dinner in Banff. We ordered steak dinners with a glass of wine, reflecting on the journey we'd gone through to find this house. At times it had seemed we wouldn't find a home, but here we were, on the verge of making it our own. Our celebration was quiet and brief but deeply enjoyed. We had a move to look forward to once we returned home.

Around the same time as our move to Mitchell, Manitoba, I decided to return to school for a master's degree. I left behind my pursuit of counselling psychology and chose to focus on teaching ESL again. At the time, it didn't make much sense because I had wanted to try working in the counselling field. But deep down, I felt it was what God wanted for me. I chose a path less travelled, especially considering my Indigenous background. Indigenous people commonly choose to be social workers.

I knew there would likely be some cultural barriers to overcome in the ESL field, but I placed my trust in God to guide me through it. Andy was always supportive of my decisions, and I remember expressing my nervousness when I received the acceptance letter into the master's program. Andy encouraged me, saying, "Trinity Western is in *Maclean's* magazine." And he was right. At the time, Trinity Western University was highly ranked, and I was accepted into their program with my Providence degree. Aside from being recognized in *Maclean's*, Trinity Western was based in British Columbia.

I first discovered TWU through a friend. Sarah was an ESL instructor in Winnipeg, and I was surprised to learn she had pursued her master's at Trinity Western. Her academic journey was similar to mine, and after seeing how it opened doors for her in Winnipeg schools, I thought it might be the right fit for me, too.

My studies began with a visit to the TWU campus for a couple months during the summer. Langley is on the outskirts of Vancouver city, about an hour's drive away, and has a population of roughly thirty thousand. The area has a small strip mall, a few restaurants, and a bus route connecting it to Vancouver, along with an e-rail line. Langley has two universities: Kwantlen Polytechnic and Trinity Western. TWU is a private Christian liberal arts university, established in 1962.

I expected the campus to be larger than my old college—most likely because of its mention in *Maclean's*—but it was actually similar in size. Trinity had a nice, well-kept campus, and I came to appreciate it for its charm.

During my time on campus that summer, I got to know my classmates and professors. Andy and Alistaire had stayed behind in Winnipeg, as we thought it would be more financially feasible that way. I didn't want to explain to anyone that I was on a tight budget for those two months in BC. Almost everything seemed overpriced. Groceries were high, but somehow, I managed to make do and not worry too much about money. I took the e-rail line into Vancouver once for a short trip with my friend Erica, but other than that, I didn't spend much on myself.

All my classmates had a background in teaching ESL or English to second language learners, either in Canada or abroad. Some had taught in South Korea, others in Ukraine or China. God had a way of surprising me, though, and one of those surprises came when I learned that Erica was part Inuit. I discovered this during our weekend in Vancouver, visiting the Museum of Anthropology, and it was nice to know I wasn't alone in teaching abroad as an Indigenous person.

For the next three years, our class studied mostly online, and for me, that meant studying in the basement of our house in Mitchell. Andy had moved in while I was away for the summer; he was taking care of two-year-old Alistaire and working at the same time. It didn't seem to bother him much. We'd managed to find a sitter for Alistaire while I was gone—a young married couple, close in age to us, from a First Nations church on the north side of the city. I was grateful for them because we didn't know many people who were willing to watch a toddler.

Alistaire was a typical toddler, going through all the usual phases. There wasn't much that surprised us about his behaviour at that age. He was loud and hyperactive and really enjoyed his freedom at the house. It was nice having a park right behind our yard, but sometimes it was difficult to keep Alistaire inside.

He was determined to go out on his own and didn't see any problems with it.

We often visited one of my college friends, Christina, and her husband, Martin. They also had children, and we would chat about married life and our experiences with raising toddlers. It was around this time that I realized her son was gifted. He was a bit older than Alistaire, by about a year, and I remember noticing how he could talk to his mom and express himself. Alistaire wasn't talking yet, and by the time he turned two, I started to worry about his speech development.

To help with his development, I put him into an arts-based preschool program in the nearby city of Steinbach. Steinbach is a forty-five-minute drive east of Winnipeg, and at the time, our home was a twenty-minute drive to Steinbach. The preschool was for kids aged three to five.

Alistaire didn't speak at all throughout his two years at preschool. During his first year, one of the teachers I got along with best would talk to us about how Alistaire was doing in class. I liked her, and I thought she did really well with Alistaire, especially considering his shyness.

I remember the teachers there showing him how to use sign language. At the time, I noticed him using it at home as well. He would sign "thirsty" when he wanted a drink or "I want" when he wanted something, like a toy.

One of the teachers invited me into the class for a "cultural" day to share something about Indigenous culture. I brought a little book with baby photos of Alistaire and showed them to the class. The photos showed him wrapped in his Tukobisin. I sat in front of the preschoolers and explained what it was used for, then watched as they created their own crafts. I remember the teacher putting up a craft on the wall—a face with black yarn for hair, and large eyes, a nose, and a mouth drawn on. She was talking to the class about the kids creating their own and sharing them. I heard Alistaire quietly whisper, "ugly." It turned out to be a funny and cute moment as we realized he had his own thoughts about the craft.

Eventually, Alistaire did start to speak, and we took him to a speech pathologist who helped us understand how to encourage him in this area. It was a bit of work, but she advised us to repeat phrases like, "Do you want juice?" and then say, "Say juice!" We were to keep practicing this way. So, that's what I did at home with him.

After a few years of living in Mitchell, Andy and I decided to try again for a house in Winnipeg. Our home wasn't listed very high, so it sold within a couple weeks. By then, Alistaire was getting ready to start his first year at a nearby primary school, Bonnycastle.

Although he was talking to us at home, we learned that Alistaire still wasn't speaking to his teacher or classmates. So we searched for a pediatrician who could refer us to a child development specialist. It would be a while before we understood why he wasn't talking at school.

Other than that, Alistaire did extra activities like piano lessons, skating, and swimming. His favourite turned out to be skating. Every year, I enrolled him in a skating group, but after a few years, I almost decided to stop. It was always fun buying his hockey gear, but I had noticed that the skating was getting harder. The backward skating was especially challenging for Alistaire. In my mind, I let go of my dream of having a star hockey player for a son.

As the levels got higher, the skating became more advanced. The kids, now around nine years old, had so many skills by then—they could skate backward, manoeuvre their hockey sticks, and more. But Alistaire still wanted to go, and I remember watching him all dressed up in his hockey gear, doing the same moves as everyone else, though always at the back of the line. I think he would've eventually gained enough skill to play on a team if he had continued. The COVID outbreak, however, put an end to his hockey career. By the time it was over, Alistaire had lost his confidence in skating and didn't want to return.

A similar thing happened with his piano lessons. Alistaire was progressing to a level where the hand and finger movements were getting more advanced. Again, I imagined I maybe had a famous pianist on my hands. I liked that thought because some of my favourite alternative songs featured gifted pianists. Alistaire even received informal invitations from his music school to attend private music schools. But eventually, he reached a song that was too hard for him, and out of frustration, he told us he was ready to quit.

It was a tough moment for both Andy and me. I thought, "Should we let him quit? Will he think he can always quit?" I hesitated, but watching his frustration was hard, too. So we decided to allow him to quit his piano lessons. He had such a good piano teacher—Joe, who reminded us of the lead actor,

Jack Black, from *School of Rock*. He was just a talented guy with long black hair who loved music. In the end, I tried to accept the loss of not having a famous pianist for a son. I told myself he could pick it up again when he got older, so there's always a small glimmer of hope for that. The same goes for his hockey skating.

Part 3
SUMMER/NĪPIN

Chapter 8
TRIP TO THE STATES

After we sold the house in Mitchell, we used a portion of the earnings to pay off debt and with the leftover money, planned a trip to the United States. At this point, I was finishing my graduate studies. I'd barely had a summer, and it was already September when we left for Las Vegas. Vegas had low hotel rates at the time, making it a reasonable option for sightseeing. We had never been to Vegas before, and Andy was excited to travel in the States.

Our plan was to drive to Minnesota, stay a couple nights for shopping, and then take a budget flight from there to Las Vegas. In Vegas, we stayed at the Desert Rose Resort, where we spent most of our time except for evening walks along the Vegas Strip to take in the sights.

On the last day of our trip, we took a bus tour to the Grand Canyon. The tour included a stop at the Hoover Dam Bypass before continuing on to the Grand Canyon National Park. Grand Canyon was breathtaking, and we paused to take photos of the views. In the souvenir shops, I bought some T-shirts for the family and a small porcelain doll of a little boy sleeping on a drum. I especially appreciated learning about the tribes living nearby in the Canyon area. Some of my pictures are snaps of the signage for each tribe at the Eagle Point: Havasupai, Hopi, and Navajo. As I walked around, the store clerk mentioned to me that it wasn't a particularly good day for pictures because the monsoon season was just starting. The wind that day had shut down the walkway, another popular tourist attraction.

During our Grand Canyon visit, Alistaire started feeling unwell, so I gave him a Tylenol. He slept through most of our time there, but he seemed unusually sick and lethargic, and I felt we should get him to a doctor. As the tour bus prepared to head back to Vegas, we asked if there was a nearby town where we could find a doctor. Eventually, we got off the tour bus right on the main highway and took a taxi to the nearest town.

We ended up in a small town called Kingman, located in northwestern Arizona. Kingman boasts the Route 66 Museum, which has become a landmark. That evening, we spent several hours in the ER. Alistaire's test results showed he'd developed pneumonia. It was a surprise because he'd seemed fine up until the last day of our trip. We left the hospital in the middle of the night, antibiotic prescription in hand. Relieved that we'd been able to get him the necessary medical care, we were also grateful for the travel insurance we'd purchased before the trip. We put it to good use while visiting Arizona.

The three of us caught a taxi to the Greyhound bus stop, but it was past midnight and we had no idea if the buses were running that late. The taxi dropped us off at a gas station, where we sat together on the sidewalk. As we waited in the night, I couldn't help but think how upset my dad would be if he knew where we were at that hour. Eventually, we gave up on catching a Greyhound, and Andy reconnected with the taxi company to arrange a driver who was willing to take us all the way back to Las Vegas. That's how we ended up returning to the resort in the early morning hours.

We spent the last few days of our trip in Houston, Texas, with Andy's childhood friend and his family. By then, Alistaire was returning to his normal self. Andy's friend had two children, one of whom was close to Alistaire's age, so they had a great time playing together. For me, it was a chance to step away from my studies and take a much-needed break. Through all the travel and worry, we managed to make the most of the trip.

A few years later, we returned to Las Vegas with a couple of my aunts, and that experience was much better than the last. Alistaire was older, which made travelling easier, and we stayed at the lovely Cancun Resort. Most of our time was spent swimming, which Alistaire absolutely loved. I remember watching him from the sunbeds as he swam around like a little dolphin. This time, we rented a car and drove to the Grand Canyon ourselves, which was much easier than taking a bus tour. Everyone enjoyed the trip, and while the weather was hot, I found myself adjusting to the dry heat. My aunties thoroughly enjoyed the West Rim. As we visited the souvenir shops, I thought about the first time we'd travelled here—I will never forget the night we ended up in Kingman.

Chapter 9
FINISHING STUDIES

In the fall of 2014, I completed my studies at Trinity Western University. I'd spent three years studying, and when I reached the practicum stage, things became challenging. I struggled to find an educational institute willing to take me on as a student intern. When I finally found a placement, the demands of travelling back and forth from home, picking up Alistaire from the sitter, and continuing to write papers quickly became overwhelming.

Eventually, I had to quit halfway through my practicum. To complicate matters further, I applied to complete it at Providence. I started again six months later, this time teaching a summer English class at a large church in Winnipeg. It was there that I met my teaching mentor, and that church became our home church for the next ten years.

When it came time to graduate, Andy, Alistaire, my dad, and I flew from Winnipeg to Vancouver. We rented a car and stayed in a hotel close to Langley—not in Vancouver, even though it offered more to do—because I was concerned Alistaire might get tired during the graduation ceremony and need to return to the hotel. Amazingly, he sat through the entire ceremony without issue.

After the ceremony, everyone dispersed to their own dinner plans and celebrations. I had received an invitation to the Indigenous graduate dinner, which is where the four of us went. There, I met another Indigenous graduate, Katie, who was from the Haida tribe in BC. It was the first time we'd met, but we instantly connected. We both understood the immense amount of work it took to earn a degree. Hers was a master's in leadership.

Following the dinner, there was a small Indigenous tradition to honour us graduates with a blanket ceremony. The blankets Katie and I received were made of flannel, covered in bright-orange and yellow with black patterns. Each of us shared our journey to Trinity Western University. I spoke about my uncertainty over where my path would lead after earning my master's degree, but I shared that I trusted in God to guide me.

The blanket ceremony was an unexpected surprise—it wasn't mentioned as part of the graduate dinner. It made me feel truly acknowledged and was much more meaningful than I could have anticipated. It was one of those moments in my life where I've felt God's love deeply. Until that moment, I hadn't fully understood why I was led to study at TWU. But after all the struggles and sleepless nights, I finally realized the purpose behind it all.

Chapter 10
AFTER GRADUATION

Once again, we returned to house hunting in Winnipeg. Instead of looking at older homes, we decided to build. At the time, a new neighbourhood in southwest Winnipeg was undergoing significant development. Model homes had been built for viewing, so we walked through them to explore our options and determine the right fit for our price range. Eventually, we decided on a bilevel bungalow with three bedrooms and two bathrooms. The living and dining areas were open concept, giving the house a spacious feel as you entered. Andy happened to know one of the realtors, which helped us in making arrangements to build and purchase the house.

The waiting period was a year, from the initial down payment to the final sale. In the meantime, however, meeting with the interior designer was a highlight. She guided us through choosing our colour options for the kitchen cabinetry, as well as the style of fixtures and flooring. The anticipation was exciting. During the construction, the three of us often drove by the site to watch the house come together. We'd sit together on the stairs, imagining our family settled into our new home.

By early summer of 2019, the house was ready for us to move in. The neighbourhood was still under development, so we only had one neighbour with a completed home; on the other side was an empty lot. The day we moved in, Andy and I sat on the steps and prayed for God's blessing over our new home. Afterward, we had a small celebration on the front porch, sitting in our two chairs and discussing our plans for the house.

Gradually, we worked on the front yard, planting shrubs and rose bushes. It quickly became my favourite project, especially as the bright-pink roses grew larger each year, framing the front of the house beautifully.

The backyard, however, was a different story. For a long time, it remained a simple, open parking pad. Eventually, we added some rocks and a small vegetable garden, but it wasn't much to look at. It took five years—and a house loan—for us to finally build a garage.

For the first couple years, it felt like we were living with construction workers. The following year, the empty lot next to us was filled, and a new house went up.

So we lived through the usual challenges of a developing neighbourhood—the dug-up ground, tractors coming and going, and porta-potties stationed on the front sidewalk. It was all part of the process. Our neighbour mentioned that she'd been watching the construction and noticed my cat, Mickey, perched in the basement window, observing it all. Mickey was a black-and-white cat who had joined our family the previous year.

My teaching career began modestly, with a few substitute teaching jobs here and there. It took several job interviews to reestablish myself in the field. My ultimate goal, of course, was to teach at the university level.

About a year after graduation, I received an invitation to interview at University of Manitoba. As a new graduate, I had built up some strong references during my internship, and my teaching mentor—who was a lead instructor at the university—had been a key supporter.

I remember preparing carefully for the interview, dressing in my best black dress pants, a dark-red blouse, heels, and my usual straightened hair. The interview turned out to be a positive experience, not nearly as intimidating as I had anticipated.

When I got the callback offering me the position, I was overjoyed. It felt like a dream come true. Teaching at a Canadian university, with a fair salary, was everything I had hoped for. I saw this achievement as the end of my long season of chasing down supplementary work.

In hindsight, I realize I was a bit naive. I assumed my career path would align seamlessly with those of my peers—friends who had earned the same degree and had similar teaching backgrounds.

That being said, I was assigned to teach an academic listening and speaking class to a wonderful group of about twenty students. The students were primarily of Chinese descent, and given my work experience in China, it was an ideal fit for a newly graduated teacher. Overall, the teaching experience went very well. My students generally loved me, and I truly enjoyed the work. If I could have stayed, I would have.

Around this same time, however, I began to fully recognize my struggle with anxiety. Andy had always known about it and frequently encouraged me to address the issue, but I'd never realized how significant it was. Yet here I was, finally immersed in my career and enjoying teaching again, but struggling with the anxiety that had resurfaced.

At the end of the term, I faced one of my most nerve-wracking moments: a classroom observation and performance review by my supervisor. I was incredibly nervous. I remember coming to class that day and doing my best to appear calm and collected, even though I was panicking internally.

I had prepared a well-thought-out lesson that involved listening to sample lectures and highlighting key words for practice. It would have been perfect—except for one unforeseen issue. My computer wouldn't set up properly. Afterward, I realized I had unknowingly pressed a button on the university-provided laptop, a button that disabled the audio.

With no audio for the listening practice, I had to adapt on the spot, explaining the situation to my students and supervisor. Fortunately, my supervisor was understanding and took the mishap in stride. Later, she messaged me to say she wouldn't be submitting a performance review since my lesson was incomplete. She'd decided not to provide any feedback but planned to return for a second observation. While this would have been an opportunity to improve, my anxiety took over, and I avoided scheduling the follow-up observation and feedback session.

During the last month of the fall term, I focused on preparing my students for their CELPIP (Comprehensive English

Language Proficiency Index Program) exams. I convinced both my supervisor—and myself—that regular lessons weren't necessary because we were primarily reviewing notes by that point. Once exam week had ended, my supervisor handed out the instructors' "end-of-term tasks," which included completing a reflection. I felt defeated as I left the university that day. I hadn't completed a second observation or received full performance feedback, and I left my term reflection incomplete.

Shortly afterward, I began searching for another teaching role—not because I wasn't hired back, but because my contract had ended. I later learned from coworkers that the ESL program didn't have a consistent demand for part-time instructors. This reality dashed my hopes of securing a full-time position as a university instructor.

I transitioned to working as a part-time instructor, which wasn't difficult given my master's degree in TESOL. By then, I was confident in my ability to secure teaching work, but the new challenge was in finding a stable, full-time position that didn't depend on contract renewals.

For the next five years, I continued to take on part-time instructor roles, primarily in academic settings. This allowed me to build valuable experience while also providing the flexibility I needed to pursue other personal goals. I worked on managing my anxiety and eventually set my sights on future professional development opportunities.

Part 4
FALL/TAKWĀKIN

Chapter 11
DEALING WITH ANXIETY

Following the completion of another college teaching contract, I found myself with some free time to focus on personal growth. I decided to join an evening class designed for individuals dealing with anxiety. Organized by a group that specialized in anxiety disorders, the class ran for eight weeks, and each session focused on strategies to address anxious thought patterns. We were provided with a guidebook and weekly tasks to complete.

This experience was valuable because it allowed me to connect with others who struggled with anxiety and see how it affected them personally. I learned how to challenge my thought processes, something I hadn't effectively done before. This newfound understanding helped me address obstacles that had previously impacted my career.

Around this time, I also decided to pursue further professional development. I felt I could build useful skills in the administrative field, so I enrolled in evening human resources classes at the University of Manitoba. Alongside my studies,

I volunteered in an HR department at a local shelter, gaining hands-on experience.

I vividly remember my final teaching position. Similar to my last teaching role in China, it was one of the most memorable experiences of my career. The workplace had a more relaxed atmosphere, offering me the flexibility I needed for lesson planning. It was a position at an adult learning centre, within the school division. During the day, I worked with newcomer adults who had a lower level of English proficiency, and in the evenings, I taught a mid-to-higher-level class. One of my favourite moments was introducing Indigenous topics to my evening class. Because the students were at a higher level (Benchmark 5), it was easier to discuss subjects related to Indigenous Canadian history.

The timing was ideal, as new teaching materials had recently become available for adult newcomers to Canada. I incorporated topics such as Indigenous Treaties, the Royal Proclamation, and the Truth and Reconciliation Commission. As much as possible, I wanted to shed light on the complete story Canada's history, which is so often overlooked. When I first introduced this material, it was surprising—but perhaps not entirely unexpected—when my students would ask me, "Where are the Indigenous Peoples?" So often, they were uninformed of the community they lived in or the Indigenous culture that surrounded them.

For one lesson, I arrived early to print the student worksheets and finalize my lesson plan. However, something had gone wrong and I couldn't print my materials. Sitting in the teachers' room, I felt my anxiety building to a slow but inevitable panic attack. As my coworkers came in to prepare for their own classes, I muttered aloud, "I'm going to lose my job tonight." I imagined my students running to the program manager to complain about their teacher's lack of preparation and their boredom during the three-to-four-hour lesson.

A coworker noticed my distress and asked about my lesson plan. When I explained that the topic was Indigenous history, she suggested having the students work on an autobiography exercise. Inspired by her idea, I decided to focus on Justice Murray Sinclair. I quickly found an autobiography template on the school computer, printed it out, and used it to pivot the evening's lesson.

Despite my nerves, I managed to remain calm and composed in front of the class. I told the students we would continue exploring Indigenous topics and handed out the materials I had just prepared. The class spent the evening researching Justice Murray Sinclair, Canada's first Indigenous Canadian judge. To my relief, they seemed genuinely interested in the activity. By the end of the evening, one of my students looked up and said, "He has a very interesting life… it's not fair that I haven't heard about him before. He's accomplished so much." He reflected on the fact that Canadian society can often be unfair, noting that Sinclair deserved far more recognition.

In that moment, I was glad for the "unplanned" lesson. If I hadn't lost my original materials, my coworker might not have suggested the autobiography exercise. Sometimes the most meaningful teaching moments happen spontaneously, and this was one of them.

Shortly afterward, COVID-19 hit and all classroom plans transitioned to online learning. A year later, all instructors were required to interview before they returned to teaching. I decided not to reapply due to the uncertainties surrounding the pandemic. Though I didn't return for another year, I left knowing I had done my part and, most importantly, had managed not to "lose my job" that night.

As I considered my professional future, I decided to pivot toward program development, enrolling in Program Development for Adult Learners at University of Manitoba. I balanced my studies with part-time teaching in the public school system. This decision stemmed from my growing frustration with the short-term contracts in teaching—I wanted stability and a more consistent career path.

Near the end of my studies, I began applying for roles in program development and eventually found work as an instructional designer. This transition marked a new chapter in my professional life, one that allowed me to blend my teaching expertise with a more structured and stable career.

Chapter 12
NEW CHALLENGES

Once the COVID pandemic had subsided, life at home felt different—and not necessarily for the better. One of our biggest challenges was Alistaire's struggle to recover from the disruption of the pandemic. His motivation and attitude seemed to plummet, and getting him back into a regular school routine became a constant battle. At the same time, tensions surfaced in my relationship with Andy. The challenges with Alistaire and other pressures took their toll, and eventually, we decided to take a break. Andy moved into a small apartment for a few months.

During that time, Andy and I tried to stay connected for Alistaire's sake. I remember the walks we took as a family, discussing possible solutions to the stress we were all feeling. Andy suggested that maybe a fresh start in a new home could help, and for a while, we seriously considered it. While he focused on finding homes within Winnipeg, I thought a bigger move might provide the change we needed. I suggested relocating to Toronto or Vancouver, imagining the opportunities and new beginnings such a move could bring.

We started browsing homes online, particularly in the Toronto area. We even contacted realtors and mapped out a tentative plan to sell our house and use the proceeds to relocate. However, as we moved forward, it became clear that Andy wasn't ready to let go of our current home. Our plans to relocate gradually fizzled; shortly afterward, Andy and I decided to separate again.

This time, however, Andy didn't move out. We stayed in the same house for a short period as I adjusted to the demands of my new role in instructional design. This new chapter in my career marked a significant transition. I was finally stepping away from the uncertainty of contract teaching positions and into a full-time administrative role. The job offered flexible hours, remote work opportunities, and a chance to gain experience in educational programming at a higher level.

My new position was with an adult education institute that served Indigenous communities across northern Ontario. It felt deeply rewarding to contribute to an organization that aligned so closely with my roots, and I was certainly familiar with the unique challenges of the region. I found the work itself engaging—I was responsible for developing courses and collaborating with colleagues who shared my passion for education.

This was a refreshing change from the fast-paced, and sometimes unpredictable, nature of the ESL field. For the first time in years, it seemed I was in the right place, professionally and personally. Though my home life was still in flux, this new role provided the sense of stability and purpose I had been seeking for years.

During the winter months, the three of us planned a much-needed trip to Mexico over Christmas break. We travelled to Puerto Vallarta, a charming coastal city on the west coast of Mexico. The city was beautiful. Its sunlit beaches, old-style homes, and cobblestone roads exuded character and history.

In the evenings, we strolled along the beach, letting the sound of the waves wash over us. The resort was lovely, though Alistaire was initially shy in the open-air restaurant because of the birds sneaking around for food. After a couple days, however, he warmed up and began exploring the resort on his own. The staff was friendly and the food was incredible, making the experience even more special.

One of my favourite parts of travelling is supporting local businesses, so I spent time wandering through town in search of souvenirs. I picked up some beautiful jewellery: a pearl bracelet with a charm, a silver bracelet with a crystal cross, and a set of gold-trimmed rings shaped like the sun. The sun became a symbol of Puerto Vallarta to me, as it shone brightly during most of our trip.

After dinner, our family often enjoyed live performances at the resort. Each show featured a different singer, but one performance stood out above the rest. On one of our last nights, close to New Year's Eve, a woman dressed in traditional attire sang mariachi songs. Later, she went around offering tequila shots to anyone willing to try. When it was my turn, she poured tequila straight into my mouth, spilling a little in the process—it was a moment of laughter and fun.

When we weren't shopping or enjoying the entertainment, I took full advantage of the sunshine, lounging on tanning beds and soaking up the warmth.

The return to Canada was a stark contrast—cold winter weather greeted us immediately. Shortly after our return, I found a new apartment and began preparing to move out. Living alone felt like the right decision, though I think Andy was taken aback by how quickly it all unfolded. After I moved out, he brought me coffee and told me he didn't want us to break up.

At that point, though, it felt like it was too little, too late. The challenges we'd faced with Alistaire, as well as in our relationship, had taken their toll. We began the process of working on a separation agreement, which eventually led to a final divorce.

Selling the house we'd built together was a long and emotional process. It took about a year to finalize, and it wasn't an ideal time to sell. Despite that, we made every effort to prepare the house for showings. Andy hired a cleaning service, and we tackled small projects—like replacing the carpets and updating the en suite bathroom. The garage had become a storage space for unused items, and it was finally sorted, with many things donated to thrift stores.

Through it all, we lived separately and managed to coparent Alistaire, dividing our time with him as fairly as possible

Chapter 13
MOTHERHOOD

During these times of change within our family, Alistaire began exploring new interests. Eventually, he decided to change his name to Kai, reflecting his need for self-evolvement. His newfound passion for acting seemed to stem from his love of action movies. For months, he expressed a strong desire to visit Los Angeles, a place he viewed as the hub of his favourite stars, including Sylvester Stallone and Arnold Schwarzenegger.

After a year of persistent reminders from Kai, I decided to make his wish come true. Early that summer, we spent a week touring Los Angeles. Kai had meticulously planned the trip, spending months studying the city on Google Maps. He already had a list of must-see locations: the Hollywood Walk of Fame, Universal Studios, and the Santa Monica Pier.

We stayed at the Millennium Biltmore Hotel, a historic landmark in downtown LA. Though it wasn't close to the main tourist attractions, its charm more than made up for the distance. The hotel had a rich history, and its hallways were adorned with photos of actors and scenes from iconic films and music videos that had been shot there. I was thrilled to recognize locations from some of my favourite movies, like *Pretty in Pink* and *Splash*, as well as the swimming pool scene from *Cruel Intentions*.

Our first stop was the Hollywood Walk of Fame, where Kai excitedly searched for his favourite actors' stars. We spent hours walking up and down the famous boulevard, taking photos and soaking in the vibrant atmosphere. The area was bustling and was filled with souvenir shops, restaurants, and street performers. It was such a highlight that we visited three or four times during our stay.

The following morning, I booked a star homes tour. We woke up early and called an Uber to take us to the meeting point. The ride didn't go as planned—a simple question about the destination upset the driver, who abruptly dropped us off at an unmarked street corner. Stranded for an hour, I scrambled to reschedule our tour and book another Uber. While it was an unsettling experience, we finally made it to the tour location.

It was worth the trouble. The guide shared fascinating stories about the famous neighbourhoods of Hollywood Hills and Bel Air, detailing the histories of the luxurious homes and their celebrity owners. While many properties were hidden behind tall fences or lush greenery, the allure of these exclusive enclaves was undeniable. I managed to capture a snapshot of the iconic Hollywood sign and the legendary Beverly Hills Hotel.

Later in the trip, we spent half a day at Universal Studios. The behind-the-scenes tour was a particular highlight. It featured famous movie sets from *Jurassic Park* and *Back to the*

Future and showcased intricate model towns, houses, and even a life-size crashed airplane. The effort and detail that went into these productions was incredible.

The tour also included immersive rides inside massive tunnels. Lined with giant screens, the tunnels' intense sound effects and visuals made the experience thrilling for me, but Kai wasn't as impressed. Afterward, we wandered around the studio grounds, grabbed some snacks, and explored the new Super Mario village. Though the themed rides weren't quite his thing, we still enjoyed the time together before heading back to the Biltmore Hotel.

One of Kai's most anticipated destinations was the Santa Monica Pier. When we arrived, the pier was lively but not overly crowded. We strolled along the boardwalk, enjoyed a meal, and took photos while gazing at the ocean. The beach was pristine, and the weather was perfect for walking along the shore and dipping our feet in the water. It was a peaceful and memorable afternoon.

The trip turned out to be an incredible bonding experience for us. Kai was thrilled to explore the places he'd dreamed of, from the homes of Hollywood's elite to the bustling tourist hotspots. He left Los Angeles inspired and more determined than ever to pursue his passion for acting.

Upon returning home, Kai enrolled in an acting school that held weekly classes. Watching him take that step toward his dream filled me with pride. His excitement for acting and his willingness to work toward his goals reminded me of the importance of supporting and nurturing his aspirations.

Though the trip had its share of challenges, it was ultimately a valuable experience. Kai and I created lasting memories, and it was gratifying to see him so engaged and motivated. Our time in Los Angeles was more than just a journey to a city of stars. It was a journey toward Kai discovering his dreams and finding his path.

Chapter 14
FUTURE GOALS

O ne area I've always tried to grow in, especially after some of my struggles with Kai, is in being a good mom. It took a long time to work with the schools, and it was a lengthy process to determine whether he needed support. Navigating the string of meetings, waiting for referrals, and receiving advice was important, but so was maintaining my own personal health in order to be present for my son. I feel fortunate because he was willing to travel with me during his early teen years, a time when teens usually don't like to be seen around adults as much. Part of being his parent is supporting his goals and helping him prepare for whatever choices he'll need to make to accomplish them.

Another area I want to focus on is continuing the work I feel my path is guiding me toward—using the skills I've acquired from teaching, administration, and volunteer work.

When I imagine myself in retirement, a couple scenarios come to mind regarding the "where"—but whether God will allow this is another matter. One dream I have is to retire and return to Southeast Asia, possibly to build a home for Kai and me, somewhere we can enjoy the warm weather and nearby beaches. But what's most important is that I will be serving others and sharing the love of God wherever I live, whether it be in Canada or abroad.

EPILOGUE

In one of my many conversations with our expat friends in China, we had a discussion about a fellow teacher who had passed away. The teacher was older in age and had perhaps decided to teach after his retirement. He had passed on during the holidays, and his employer at the time was left to handle the aftermath. Maybe this teacher enjoyed teaching so much that he wanted to leave this earth in that way, transitioning into the spirit realm. But for myself, I wonder who would intentionally choose to pass away so far from their childhood home and family.

Sometimes during the fall season, my dad comes out to the city to visit. Often, Dad, Kai, and I go out for supper to a restaurant, and I tell him some stories from my travels. One such time, I mentioned the story about the old teacher. My Dad sat quietly as I explained how the employer had to take care of the teacher afterward. Dad often does that when it is a serious topic.

Since I was a young Oji-Cree teenager, my faith has been a part of me—through adulthood and through all the ups and downs. I've always felt this was part of my purpose: travelling and working where I feel led to be and creating relationships with the people I encounter, whether it is in Canada or abroad. My home is where I am placed, although temporarily—my focus is not on the physical gains but on the spiritual. So, while it's a less popular scenario for a teacher to pass away while abroad, it has always made sense to me because the teacher was doing what he loved.

THE END

*Kindergarten school photo, St. Martin School,
1988 in Thunder Bay, ON*

*Myself and friend Elisabet on missions trip
in Johannesburg, South Africa, 1999*

High School graduation photo at Mount St. Joseph's College,
in Sault Ste. Marie, ON, 2000

Myself on the Great Wall in Beijing, China, 2000

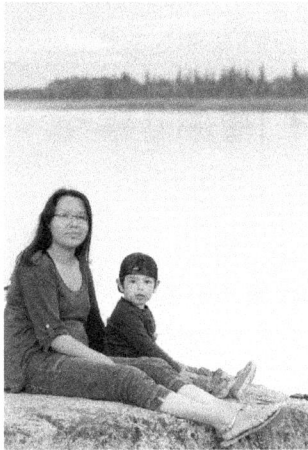

Myself and son Alistaire taken in Bearskin Lake, ON, 2012

Graduated with Master's degree in TESOL
at Trinity Western University, in Langley, BC, 2014